THE SECRET WORLD OF

Prairie Dogs

THE SECRET WORLD OF

Prairie Dogs

John Woodward

 Raintree

Chicago, Illinois

© 2004 Raintree
Published by Raintree, a division of Reed Elsevier, Inc.
Chicago, Illinois
Customer Service 888-363-4266
Visit our website at www.raintreelibrary.com

Project Editors: Geoff Barker, Marta Segal Block, Rebecca Hunter, Jennifer Mattson
Production Manager: Brian Suderski
Consultant: Michael Chinery
Designed by Ian Winton
Illustrated by Robert Morton
Planned and produced by Discovery Books

Printed and bound in the United States by Lake Book Manufacturing, Inc.
07 06 05 04 03
10 9 8 7 6 5 4 3 2 1

Library of Congress Cataloging-in-Publication Data:
Woodward, John, 1954-
Prairie dogs / John Woodward.
v. cm. -- (The secret world of)
Includes bibliographical references and index.
Contents: Burrowing squirrels -- Prairie dog society -- Home on the range -- Food and feeding -- Reproduction -- Dangers and defenses -- Prairie neighbors -- Threats and conservation.
ISBN 0-7398-7025-4 (lib. bdg.-hardcover)
1. Prairie dogs--Juvenile literature. [1. Prairie dogs.] I. Title.
II. Series.
QL737.R68W68 2003
599.36'7--dc21

2003002290

Acknowledgments
The publisher would like to thank the following for permission to reproduce photographs:
p.8, 11, 14, 15, p.31 (top) Frank Lane Picture Agency; p.9 E & D Hosking/Frank Lane Picture Agency; p.10 (top) Mills Tandy/Oxford Scientific Films; p.10 (bottom), 21, 27 (top), 32, 33, 34, 35, 39 (top and bottom) Corbis; p.12, 31 (bottom) Wendy Shattil & Bob Rozinski/Oxford Scientific Films; p.13 Stouffer Enterprises Inc/Oxford Scientific Films; p.16, 24 Martyn Colbeck/Oxford Scientific Films; p.18, 27 (bottom) Martyn Chillmaid/Oxford Scientific Films; p.20 L West/Frank Lane Picture Agency; p.22 Jorg & Petra Wegner/Bruce Coleman; p.23 Rod Planck/Natural History Photographic Agency; p.25 Hans Reinhard/ Bruce Coleman; p.26 John Cancalosi/Bruce Coleman; p. 28, 37, 41 Rich Kirchner/Natural History Photographic Agency; p.. 29 David C. Fritts/Oxford Scientific Films; p. 30 T Kitchin & V Hurst//Natural History Photographic Agency; p.36, 40 Stephen Krasemann/Natural History Photographic Agency; p.38 D Kinzler/Frank Lane Picture Agency; p.42 (top) J C Allen/ Frank Lane Picture Agency; p.42 (bottom) Mark Newman/Frank Lane Picture Agency; p.43 Michael Fogden/Oxford Scientific Films.

Other acknowledgments
Cover: Joe McDonald/Bruce Coleman

Note to the Reader
Some words are shown in bold, **like this.** You can find out what they mean by looking in the glossary.

Contents

CHAPTER 1
Burrowing Squirrels

 Scientists believe that there are about 4,000 different species of mammals, and nearly half of them are various types of rodents. About 260 of these rodent species are squirrels of some kind—a group that includes the prairie dog.

 In the centuries before the colonization of the Great Plains by ranchers and farmers, there were about 5.5 billion prairie dogs living on the grasslands.

 The most common species, the black-tailed prairie dog, is 14–17 in. (35–43 cm) long, and weighs 2–3 lb (0.9–1.4 kg).

Prairie dogs in captivity have been known to live for eight years, but wild ones rarely survive for more than four years.

A prairie dog is actually a ground squirrel, a type of squirrel that spends its whole life on the ground—or under it—instead of in the trees. Other ground squirrels include chipmunks, sousliks, and marmots. Their tails are shorter and not as bushy as those of tree squirrels, because a bushy tail would be too bulky to fit inside a **burrow.** Many ground squirrels also have smaller ears than tree squirrels. This is so that their ears do not get in the way when they are burrowing underground.

Prairie dogs are **mammals,** which are **endothermic** animals that feed their young on milk until they are old enough to digest other types of food. Endothermic (warm-blooded) animals can warm themselves up or cool themselves down to keep their body at the right temperature. This is unlike **ectothermic** (or cold-blooded) animals, such as insects and reptiles, whose bodies stay at the same temperature as their surroundings.

▶ With its sharp front teeth for gnawing and its small furry body, a prairie dog is a typical rodent, the group of animals that includes mice and squirrels. A prairie dog is basically a squirrel with a short tail.

Mammals include a wide variety of creatures, including wolves, horses, whales, and people. But almost half of the different **species** of mammals on the planet are **rodents.** Rodents eat mainly by nibbling and gnawing tough plants and seeds. They include rats, mice, squirrels, and prairie dogs.

Eyes
A prairie dog has very good eyesight, and its eyes are set high on the sides of its head for a wider range of vision.

Ears
The ears are smaller than those of tree squirrels, so they do not get in the way when the animal is underground.

Whiskers
Sensitive whiskers allow the prairie dog to feel its way through its dark burrow.

Front teeth
The front teeth are self-sharpening, and keep growing throughout the prairie dog's life.

Legs
Short, strong legs are ideal for burrowing underground.

Feet
A prairie dog has big, powerful feet with an extra-long claw on each "thumb."

Tail
Although short, the tail is useful for signaling to other prairie dogs.

CHISEL TEETH

The reason **rodents** have managed to spread all over the world and live in so many different ways is largely due to their unusual teeth. Human teeth are covered with a hard material called **enamel,** which stops them from wearing out too quickly. But the four front teeth of a rodent like a prairie dog are coated with enamel only on the front surface. This means that the back of each tooth wears down faster than the front, creating a sharp blade like a carpenter's chisel.

A beaver—one of the biggest rodents—can use these chisel teeth to cut down trees, but prairie dogs use them to chew grass and plants.

The chisel teeth stay sharp because the back surface is worn down by constant nibbling. But the teeth never wear out completely, because they never stop growing. The front teeth of some rodents grow nearly a quarter of an inch (6 millimeters) every week.

Rodents also have tough back teeth for chewing, with ridges of hard enamel for grinding food to a pulp. Since these teeth are not used for cutting, they are not designed to wear down to a sharp edge like the front teeth. They stop growing when the animal is **mature**— just as your teeth do.

A prairie dog's four front teeth are very different from its back teeth. The front teeth stay sharp and never wear out because they are constantly growing.

USEFUL GAP

Prairie dogs and other rodents have a big gap between the front and back teeth called the **diastema.** A prairie dog can draw its lips into this to seal its mouth off from its front teeth. A **burrowing** prairie dog finds this very useful when it is digging,

As this black-tailed prairie dog digs its burrow, it may hack at hard dirt with its front teeth as well as its sharp claws.

because it can loosen earth with its teeth without getting a mouthful of dirt. However, prairie dogs mainly burrow using their short, powerful legs with their strong feet and sharp claws.

GRASSLAND HOME

Prairie dogs live mainly on the prairies, the grasslands that once covered all of the midwestern and western states. Today most of the prairies have been turned into farmland or pastures for **grazing** cattle. The **native** prairie grasses and other plants have been plowed under, and most of the prairie dogs have disappeared. But they can still be found in a few places where some original grasses and plants survive.

Like all prairie dogs, the white-tailed prairie dog holds grasses in its front feet as it nibbles them. This allows it to keep watch for danger while it feeds.

▲ Storm clouds darken the sky over a surviving patch of prairie in Texas. Most of these native American grasslands have now been plowed under to grow crops or grass for cattle.

FIVE VARIETIES

There are five different kinds of prairie dog, and most scientists agree that they are separate **species.** These five different types have different habits and do not mate with each other.

The Gunnison's prairie dog has a much shorter tail than the others. It lives in the high valleys of the Rocky Mountains in the Four Corners region, where the states of Utah, Colorado, New Mexico, and Arizona meet. Utah is also the home of the Utah prairie dog, the smallest species. Utah prairie dogs are now very scarce, but are not as rare as the Mexican prairie dog, which is found in only a few parts of Mexico.

The most common and widespread species is the black-tailed prairie dog, which lives on the dry plains from Mexico to Canada. Its tail has a black tip, unlike that of the white-tailed prairie dog, which lives in the western United States on higher land in places like Colorado, Utah, Wyoming, and Montana. This book will tell you mostly about the black-tailed prairie dog and how it lives.

Barking Squirrels

Prairie dogs got their name because of the way they bark in alarm when they sense danger. This was first described by the explorer Meriwether Lewis, who was part of the expedition led by Lewis and William Clark to cross the Great Plains in the early 1800s. In 1804 Lewis was camping near the Missouri River when he wrote of vast numbers of barking squirrels on the prairies. Later, they became known as "prairie dogs"—a name that has caused many people to confuse them with coyotes over the years.

CHAPTER 2
Prairie Dog Society

Prairie dogs spend a lot of time picking dirt and insects out of other prairie dogs' fur. This gets rid of fleas, ticks, and other bloodsucking bugs, but it also helps the animals to get to know each other.

When young males live together, one male usually dominates the others. He is usually the first to find a mate and start a family.

The largest prairie dog families have been known to cover up to an acre (0.4 hectare), about the size of a football field. Each community might be made up of several such families.

Many **mammals** live in social groups. Usually these are based around the family, although these families are often much bigger than ours. A wolf pack, for example, is an extended family group centered on a breeding male and female and their pups, as well as pups from previous years. A herd of wild horses has one male, three or four females, their foals, and their young from previous years.

COTERIES, TOWNS, AND CITIES

Prairie dog society is also based on extended family groups, known as **coteries.** They are like wild horse herds, with one adult male who

A prairie dog coterie is really a big family of closely related animals, who live together and protect each other. These prairie dogs are looking out for danger.

usually mates with about four females, each of whom produces up to eight pups every year. The pups stay with their parents for at least two years, so a coterie can easily have more than 50 prairie dogs of different ages.

The coteries themselves live together in societies called **wards.** Although the coteries of a ward form a close-knit neighborhood in which the animals all cooperate to watch out for enemies, the members of each coterie stay in their own **burrow** systems for much of the year. Neighboring

Although each coterie has its own burrow system, it always lives near other coteries to form a busy neighborhood. This prairie dog is watching for trouble while others feed.

wards form prairie dog towns or even cities. The wards of each town are often separated by barriers such as roads or belts of trees, but are usually within sight and sound of each other.

Compared with many mammals, prairie dogs have a very highly organized society. They do everything in the company of neighbors, and a prairie dog is never lonely.

13

Good Neighbors

Prairie dogs are most loyal to the other members of their families **(coteries)** and usually are friendly with the other coteries in their larger neighborhoods **(wards).** All the prairie dogs within a coterie are welcome inside the family **burrow** system. But if they stray into the burrows of a neighboring coterie they are sometimes driven out by the resident male. There may be some rivalry with other wards in the prairie dog town, but not much. Some prairie dogs may even move from one part of town to another. Friendliness between neighbors

Two black-tailed prairie dogs gently touch their noses and front teeth as they greet each other on the flower-covered prairies of Colorado. Close contact gives them a good chance to recognize friends and detect intruders.

changes with the seasons. In the fall and winter the breeding males get jealous of rivals, and defend their coteries against **trespassing** males. Because of this, the coteries close their doors to each other throughout the colder months. But in spring they relax, and by summer neighboring coteries spend a lot of time **socializing.**

NEW BLOOD

Young male prairie dogs eventually leave their home coteries, and join other males in nonbreeding coteries. Young females may do the same before eventually teaming up with males. The females usually stay close to home, but males may leave to join other wards in the town. The arrival of new members to a coterie is important. The newcomers ensure that related prairie dogs do not always breed among themselves. Such **inbreeding** can cause problems, and it is one reason why isolated populations of animals often become unhealthy and die out.

Prairie Dog Language

Prairie dogs often seem to "kiss" each other as they touch noses in greeting. They probably use this as a way of recognizing their family and neighbors. But they also have a surprisingly complex language, with at least eleven types of calls and many different gestures. Some experts believe that prairie dog language is as complex as the language of dolphins, which are some of the most intelligent, sociable animals on the planet.

I DIDN'T KNOW THAT

15

CHAPTER 3
Home on the Range

A prairie dog town is a maze of **burrows** and chambers with many entrances. The town does not usually look like much from the surface: just a lot of holes surrounded by mounds of bare earth and closely cropped grass. But underneath lies an interesting example of animal house design.

Each prairie dog **coterie** digs and looks after its own network of burrows, and any member can use any part of the network. The burrow system is the coterie's **territory,** like a family house, although residents may allow visitors. The lead male prairie dog has the job of challenging any strangers and chasing them out if necessary—however, he is often helped by one of the adult females.

 The biggest prairie dog towns are those of the black-tailed prairie dog, which is also the most common and widespread species.

 Most prairie dog towns are in short-grass plains, away from areas of tall grass and brush. This is partly because the prairie dogs avoid tall plants, and partly because their constant nibbling keeps the plants from growing.

Gunnison's prairie dogs, found in high valleys in the Rocky Mountains, live in much smaller colonies than other prairie dogs.

▶ A territorial male sniffs the air outside the family burrow and checks the neighborhood for strangers. Although prairie dogs are social animals, they still like to keep their burrows private.

BURROW NETWORKS

The main tunnels are 3–4 inches (7–10 centimeters) across, with funnel-shaped entrances so that the prairie dogs can dive into them easily. Each tunnel heads down at a steep angle, like a mine shaft, for 3–16 feet (1–5 meters), then levels off into a **horizontal** burrow before climbing to open out at another entrance. Side tunnels branch off from the lower burrows, leading to nest chambers and nurseries. There is often a chamber near each entrance, where a prairie dog can sit and listen for danger above ground before risking a quick look.

GOING UNDERGROUND

The burrow network is complicated, consisting of many chambers linked by tunnels. There are two entrances to keep air flowing and to provide an exit route in case any **predators** enter the system.

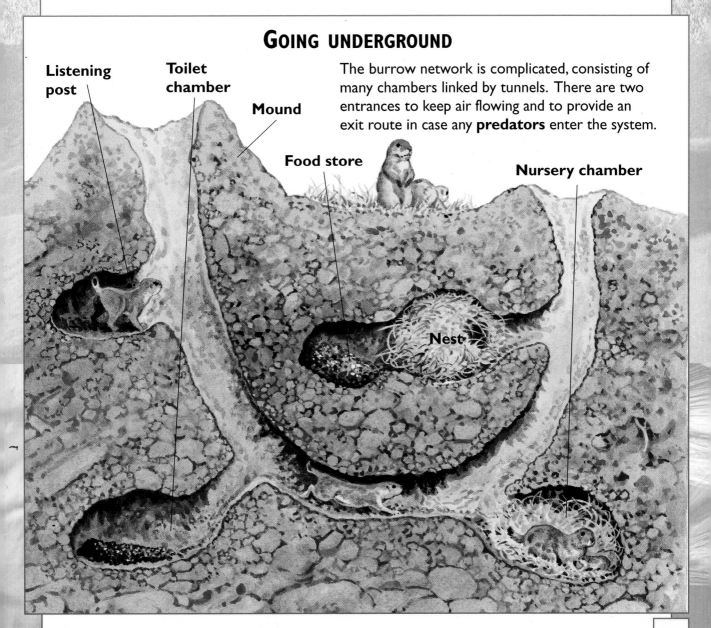

Listening post

Toilet chamber

Mound

Food store

Nursery chamber

Nest

LOOKOUT POINTS

Each entrance to the **burrow** system is surrounded by a mound of earth. Some of these are low, round-topped mounds about a foot (30 centimeters) high. Others are more like steep-sided miniature volcanoes, up to about 3 feet (90 centimeters) high.

The mounds make good lookouts for the prairie dogs, allowing them to see if any **predators** are coming.

A young black-tailed prairie dog peeks out from its family's burrow. The high mound around the hole works to draw fresh air through the system of tunnels.

However, they have other, even more important functions. Even a low mound acts as a defense against the floods that often follow rainstorms on the prairies. The mound prevents water from pouring down the shaft and flooding the burrow system.

FRESH AIR

Scientists have also discovered that the tall, volcano-like mounds work like chimneys. As the breeze blows up and over them, it creates a suction effect that pulls air out of the tunnel and through the mound. The other end of this tunnel always leads to one of the low, rounded mounds, where there is no suction effect. Instead, fresh air is drawn into the tunnel to replace the air being sucked out at the chimney end. So by building mounds of different heights at each end of the main tunnels, the prairie dogs create a kind of natural air-conditioning system.

VITAL VENTILATION

As the air is drawn over a high mound by the breeze, it speeds up. This makes it drag stale air out of the burrow and pull fresh air in through the other entrance.

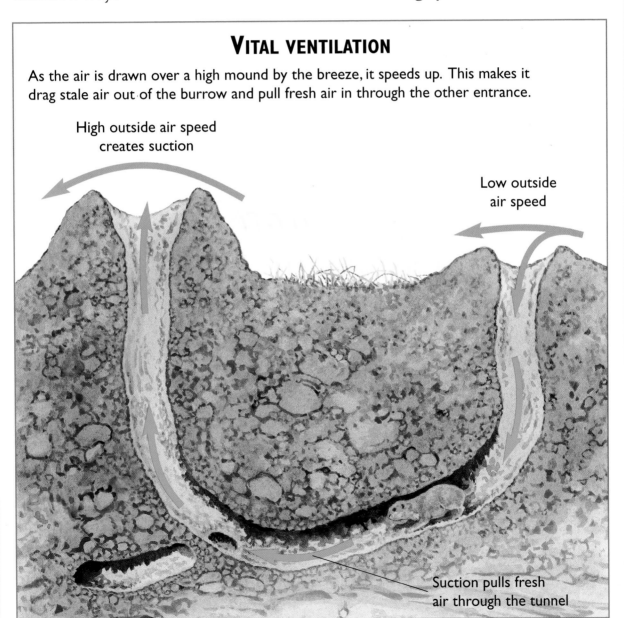

High outside air speed creates suction

Low outside air speed

Suction pulls fresh air through the tunnel

NEW TERRITORY

As the prairie dogs breed, their **burrows** can become overcrowded. If the situation gets really bad, some of the prairie dogs may have to move out. In many other animal **species,** when overcrowding occurs the younger animals leave. They frequently do not survive. Prairie dogs have a different system. The young ones stay at home, in the burrows that they know, and the older, more experienced animals leave to **colonize** new **territory.**

They rarely go far, but start digging new burrow systems on suitable ground near the old **colony.** New burrows may be separated by a ridge or creek, but they are still part of the same prairie dog town. Gradually the town gets bigger.

New burrow networks on fresh ground are always made by older prairie dogs who are experienced diggers.

In the past a typical town may have covered over 100 acres (40 hectares) —about the same as one hundred football fields put together!

BORROWERS

Sometimes prairie dogs move out of old burrows and leave them empty. They do not stay empty for long, however. Other prairie animals move in, including rats and mice, cottontail rabbits, burrowing owls, and even rattlesnakes! Some of these animals have become so used to living in former prairie dog towns that they rarely live anywhere else.

Dog City

In the days before most of the Midwest was turned into farmland, some prairie dogs lived in huge, sprawling cities that covered areas bigger than some states. One of these was discovered on the high plains of Texas in about 1900. It was about 100 miles wide and 250 miles long (160 by 400 kilometers)—an area as big as Lake Michigan! This prairie dog city had a population of maybe 400 million prairie dogs, which is more than today's entire human population of the United States, Canada, and Mexico combined.

CHAPTER 4
Food and Feeding

 To get enough protein in their diet, prairie dogs have to spend up to half of each day eating.

 Pruning by prairie dogs encourages grasses to grow in low, dense clumps, even though they would normally grow taller.

 If a prairie dog stopped wearing down its front teeth by chewing on tough plants, the teeth would would grow longer and longer, just like tusks.

The occasional insects eaten by prairie dogs supply important protein and vitamins to keep them healthy.

▶ Grass is tough on the front teeth of a prairie dog. However, because the front teeth continually grow, they never get worn down.

The favorite food of prairie dogs is grass, which is a good thing, because there is a lot of grass on the prairie. Grass accounts for about two-thirds of a prairie dog's diet, and even more in spring and early summer when the grass is lush and green. The rest of their diet consists of **forbs** (any low-growing, leafy plants other than grass), and also seeds and some insects.

Grass is usually easy to find, but it is tough on the teeth. It is peppered with tiny shards of a glasslike substance called **silica**. These shards act like sandpaper

on the teeth of grazing animals. This is not a problem for a prairie dog because of its special front teeth, which keep growing to make up for the sandpaper effect, and its big, tough back teeth, which take a long time to wear down.

CLEAR VIEW

A prairie dog usually eats by snipping off a plant with its front teeth, then holding it in its front feet while it nibbles and chews—just like a squirrel eating a nut. This method has the advantage of allowing the prairie dog to

sit upright so it can look out for danger as it feeds. A prairie dog always feeds near a **burrow** entrance so it can run for cover in an emergency. It also cuts down more plants than it can eat, biting off any tall plants so it has a clear view of any enemies nearby.

By sitting up on its hind legs, a prairie dog raises its head high above the surrounding grass. Its high-set eyes allow it to see all around, giving it a good view of anything that might spell trouble. One prairie dog always stands guard like this while the rest of the family feeds.

DAILY ROUTINE

On the dry prairies of Texas and Mexico, black-tailed prairie dogs leave their **burrows** to feed in the early morning, but then slip back underground during the heat of the day. They must not get too hot because they would lose important body moisture. Finding a drink to replace the lost moisture can be a problem on the open prairie, but as long as prairie dogs keep cool, they can get all the water they need from the plants they eat.

The prairie dogs come out to feed again in the late afternoon, and usually keep eating until sunset, when they vanish into their burrows. It is safer for prairie dogs to feed in daylight when they can still see well, rather than risk being taken by surprise in the dark.

WINTER SLEEP

In winter the plants stop growing, and prairie dogs are in danger of starvation. So they stay underground and sleep a lot to cut down on their need for food. On sunny winter afternoons, black-tailed prairie dogs come out to enjoy the fresh air and find food, but they disappear again if it gets too cold.

Although a prairie dog cannot feed in deep snow, it will come out of its burrow on a mild winter day and dig through shallow snow to find some grass.

24

Gunnison's prairie dogs that live in the Rocky Mountains and white-tailed prairie dogs in northern Wyoming have to cope with heavy snow that forces them underground for most of the winter. Some scientists think that during this time, these prairie dogs may go into a state known as **hibernation.** This is when an animal's body temperature falls and its heartbeat slows down to conserve energy. Scientists are still unsure about this, though. Prairie dogs might not actually hibernate—they may just sleep a lot during winter.

Grass Thieves?

A prairie dog eats about 2 pounds (1 kilogram) of grass and other plants every week. It takes at least 300 prairie dogs to eat as much as one cow and her calf. However, because there can be between 3,000 and 30,000 prairie dogs in a **colony,** ranchers often see them as pests that eat the grass intended for cattle. This is why ranchers frequently try to rid their land of prairie dogs.

I DIDN'T KNOW THAT

CHAPTER 5
Reproduction

Usually each pregnant female prairie dog produces between four and six young, but some may have as many as eight.

Each tiny prairie dog pup weighs only half an ounce (14 grams) when it is born.

Male Gunnison's prairie dogs are more solitary than other male prairie dogs, and do not take much part in raising the pups.

A female prairie dog has ten teats that produce milk, so her pups never have to fight for their meals.

Prairie dog **coteries** are centered around a single adult male, who lives with a group of four or five adult females (sometimes more). They mate in early spring. In Mexico this might be as early as February, but up in Canada where the winters are longer, they often mate much later, in April.

Before she has her babies, a female prairie dog collects dry grasses to line her nursery burrow and give her young a soft bed.

Baby prairie dogs are born blind, naked, and helpless. These pups are only a week old. It will take another three weeks for them to grow their fur, and another week after that before their eyes open.

10 days. By the time they are 25 days old, they have fur and are able to crawl around inside the nest chamber. Between 33 and 37 days, their eyes open. By this time they have teeth and can run around. Before long they can start exploring above ground and eating grass like their parents.

As soon as the pups can see, they are ready to find out what life is like outside the burrow and enjoy the fresh air.

Like most animals, prairie dog pups have a lot more growing to do once they are born. The females are **pregnant** for just 30 to 35 days, and their pups are born with no fur, no teeth, and with their eyes closed. They are really only half developed, but there is a very good reason for this. If the mother carried her pups for much longer, she would be too heavy to run away from danger. So she gives birth early, when her pups are just old enough to survive.

UNDERGROUND NURSERY
The tiny, naked pups are kept safe in the **burrow's** underground nursery chamber. Their mother feeds them on rich milk, and they double their birth weight within

OUT AND ABOUT

For most kinds of squirrels, child care is the job of the mother. Males show no interest at all. But prairie dogs are different. Once the pups appear above ground, both the mother and the father help look after them. They even play with them—something that helps the young animals learn the prairie dog language of calls and signals, as well as how to run, jump, and move quickly away from danger.

The pups spend a lot of time playing together in the prairie sunshine. Play makes them fit and strong, and helps them learn about life in the **coterie.**

Within a few days of leaving the den for the first time, young prairie dogs stop drinking milk and start feeding on grass and other plants. They learn which plants are the best to eat by experimenting and by watching the adults. Once they are able to look after themselves, their mother leaves the nursery and moves into another **burrow** nearby. The pups may continue to use the nursery for a few days, but eventually they leave, too, and move into any spare burrows that they can find.

WINTER SUPPLIES

By the time the young prairie dogs move into their own burrows in the fall, they are almost fully grown. They eat well to put on as much weight as possible before the winter, because if food is scarce they must survive by burning stored fat. If they run out of fat before the end of winter, they may die. But if all goes well, they will become fully **mature** in spring and will start families of their own.

Population Explosion

Prairie dogs breed quickly. A small **colony** with 30 adult males and 100 breeding females could easily produce 500 young in the spring. If half of these are female, and they all survive to have five babies the following spring, there may be 1,750 young prairie dogs dining on the grass by midsummer. After just 18 months, the colony will have grown from 130 to 2,380. And if half of these breed in the following year, they could expand the colony to over 8,000. Within a few years, the population could reach nearly 30,000! Of course, in the real world there are many factors that keep the the prairie dog population under control, such as **predators** and a limited food supply.

CHAPTER 6
Dangers and Defenses

Prairie dogs are small, plant-eating **mammals.** This makes them a favorite treat for a variety of **predators.** To a meat-eater like a fox or a big hawk, a prairie dog town is like a giant snack bar.

Some predators attack from the air, like the golden eagle, raven, and ferruginous hawk. Others attack on the ground, like the coyote, swift fox, badger, and bobcat. And a few, like the rattlesnake and the very rare black-footed ferret, may even kill prairie dogs right in their **burrows.**

 The barking alarm call of a prairie dog sounds something like "chirk—chirk—chirk," so it is sometimes called "chirking."

 Prairie dogs often have special warning barks for different types of predators. This way, the other prairie dogs know exactly what kind of animal has been spotted.

When an enemy moves away and the danger is over, prairie dogs sometimes jump for joy with their backs arched, and give a high-pitched yip.

 Although rattlesnakes sometimes kill and eat young prairie dogs, they never attack adults because they are too big to swallow.

▶ The bobcat is a stealthy killer that stalks its victims and then attacks with a sudden charge. Its deadly teeth and claws make short work of a prairie dog—if it can avoid being seen by the guards on watch.

BARKING ALARM

Prairie dogs have learned to be very cautious. Whenever they are feeding, one member of the **coterie** always stands guard on one of the high mounds at the burrow entrances. Since the whole **colony** usually feeds at once, the area is dotted with guards, all keeping watch for danger. Their eyes are set high on their head, allowing them to see in almost all directions.

Once the danger is past, a guard rears up on its hind legs, throws its head back, and gives a high yip that means, "All clear!"

If a guard spots anything suspicious, it sounds the alarm with a sharp, whistling bark, bobs up and down in excitement, calls again, then dives for cover. Within seconds all the nearby prairie dogs have vanished underground. The alarm spreads as guards farther from the danger zone begin to bark as well. This system makes it very difficult for the hunter to find a prairie dog to eat.

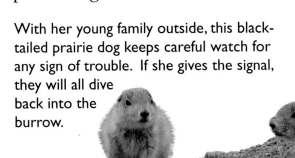

With her young family outside, this black-tailed prairie dog keeps careful watch for any sign of trouble. If she gives the signal, they will all dive back into the burrow.

31

THE BLACK-FOOTED FERRET

For thousands of years, the prairie dog's main enemy was a weasel-like animal called the black-footed ferret. With its long body, short black legs, and sharp teeth, it was perfectly equipped for hunting prairie dogs in their **burrows.** It was so good at it that it gave up hunting anything other than prairie dogs.

As long as there were millions of prairie dogs, the black-footed ferret thrived, even though each ferret needed to eat about 350 prairie

Although it was almost extinct by the 1980s, the black-footed ferret is now breeding again in the wild. However, it can only survive if the prairie dog colonies survive, too.

dogs a year. However, when people started killing prairie dogs and destroying their towns to make room for ranches and farms, the ferret suffered, too. It had almost lost the ability to hunt other animals, so when the prairie dog towns started becoming scarce, the ferrets started disappearing. By 1980 the black-footed ferret was thought to be **extinct.**

Ferret Revival

In 1981, near the small prairie town of Meeteetse, Wyoming, a rancher's dog got into a fight with a weasel and killed it. It turned out that the "weasel" was a black-footed ferret. Scientists started looking for more, and discovered a population of about 130 living wild on the prairie. Unfortunately, these ferrets were struck by a disease. As they began to die, the scientists caught as many as they could—just 18— and started breeding them in captivity. Over 1,000 black-footed ferrets bred from these few survivors have now been released back into the wild.

Microscopic Killer

Prairie dogs have an invisible enemy: a **microbe** that causes a deadly disease called **sylvatic plague.** The bug came from Asia in about 1900. It is carried by bloodsucking fleas, which pass it from one prairie dog to another. It can wipe out a whole **colony** in a few weeks.

Sylvatic plague is closely related to bubonic plague—also known as the Black Death—which killed 25 million people in Europe in the 1300s. Scientists monitor the presence of the plague in populations of prairie

dogs and other small rodents. They have to catch the animals and comb them for fleas. Then they can learn whether or not the fleas carry the plague.

CHAPTER 7
Prairie Neighbors

Many of the animals that live on the grassy plains depend on prairie dogs to make life easier for them. Their feeding habits, much like mowing, create dense, close-cropped **lawns** of grasses and other plants. These areas of shorter grasses make seeds, insects, and small animals easier to find, attracting prairie birds such as meadowlarks, grasshopper sparrows, and burrowing owls.

Baby burrowing owls build their nests in old prairie dog burrows and make a noise like a rattlesnake to scare off predators if they feel threatened.

The soil is often more fertile around a prairie dog town, because all of the animal droppings act as a natural fertilizer.

The more fertile soil around a prairie dog town encourages the growth of plants that are rare in other areas of the prairie.

Burrowing owls have unusually long legs for digging, and they often perch at the entrances to their holes. Unlike most owls, they hunt during the day.

JUICY TREAT
The constant pruning done by prairie dogs also changes the types of plants that grow around their **colonies.** Tall plants die out, and short grasses and low-growing plants replace them. As their older leaves are chewed off, the plants

sprout new, young leaves, which are juicier and easier to digest. This is good news for the prairie dogs, but also for other grazers. When vast herds of buffalo and pronghorn antelope roamed the plains, they spent a lot of time **grazing** around prairie dog lawns because they found that the grass

Before the 1800s huge herds of buffalo grazed in the prairies. Smaller herds still live on the plains and often feed on prairie dog lawns when they can find them.

tasted so much better. It was also more nutritious than the taller, tougher grass in areas that had not been kept short by prairie dogs.

DANGEROUS GUESTS

Some of the prairie dogs' neighbors move right into their towns. The burrowing owl nests underground, which is very unusual behavior for an owl. It can dig its own **burrow** if it has to, using its long legs and bill, but it prefers to use an abandoned prairie dog burrow. A prairie dog town often has burrowing owls living in burrows around its borders. The owls frequently hunt by day, catching large insects and small **mammals** like mice. They may also snatch

The prairie rattlesnake cannot dig its own burrow, so it often moves into a hole that has been made by prairie dogs. It normally feeds on small mice and ignores its prairie dog neighbors.

young prairie dogs if they can, although the prairie dog guards usually manage to stop them.

The burrows are also used by rattlesnakes, which are even less welcome. A rattlesnake can slip through a prairie dog tunnel and target a young prairie dog in the

36

dark using special heat sensors below its eyes, so its victims have trouble escaping. Most rattlers, though, are more interested in catching smaller **prey** such as mice, so the prairie dogs have learned to live with them.

NIGHT SHIFT
Cottontail rabbits may also make their homes in prairie dog towns.

Even though rabbits are not **rodents,** they have the same self-sharpening teeth as prairie dogs, and they nibble grass in the same way. But unlike prairie dogs, they prefer to feed at night, relying on their sharp hearing to warn them of danger. So when the prairie dogs stop feeding and slip into their burrows for the night, the cottontails come out for their turn.

Quality Control

Having a killer like an owl or a rattlesnake as a neighbor might seem like bad news for prairie dogs. But surprisingly, the **colony** often benefits in the long run. **Predators** usually target weak or sick animals that cannot easily escape. Strong, healthy prairie dogs generally survive and breed, so most of the young prairie dogs are likely to be strong and healthy, too.

I DIDN'T KNOW THAT

CHAPTER 8
Threats and Conservation

 Before the pioneers colonized the plains, Native American peoples hunted prairie dogs for food for at least 800 years.

 Prairie dogs are often killed by humans who regard them as pests. However, exterminating prairie dogs is not cheap. In the late 1980s, $6.2 million was spent poisoning prairie dog colonies in South Dakota.

It is illegal in Mexico to kill a Mexican prairie dog. But prairie dogs in the United States are protected only if they live on wildlife reserves.

Back in the late 1800s, when the Midwest and West were mostly wild prairie or pasture, prairie dogs were everywhere. They feasted on more than 700 million acres (280 million hectares) of grass in Montana, the Dakotas, Nebraska, Wyoming, Colorado, Utah, Kansas, Oklahoma, New Mexico, Arizona, Texas, and northern Mexico, as well as in some parts of Canada. They lived in huge prairie dog towns and cities, each one containing millions of animals.

Today, though, nearly all of the prairies have been plowed under or built over, and only a tiny fraction of the prairie dog's wild habitat survives. The largest existing prairie dog town is in the Chihuahuan Desert in Mexico. Most others have been destroyed—and not just by accident.

Huge machines have turned much of the prairie into giant wheatfields, and only a few areas of wild prairie with their original plants are left.

PEST CONTROL

Ranchers have always seen prairie dogs as pests that compete with their cattle for grass. So over the last 100 years, huge numbers have been shot and poisoned. Whole prairie dog towns have been wiped out and the land turned over to cattle or crops. The states of Nebraska and South Dakota

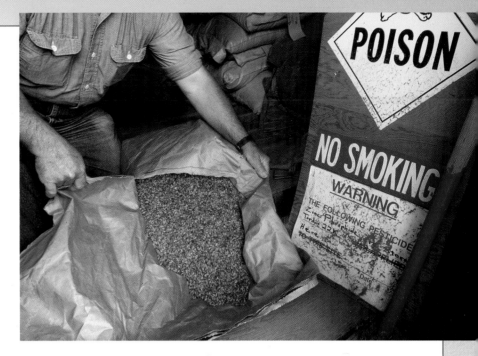

In some places, prairie dogs are still being deliberately killed by ranchers giving them poisoned food like these oats.

have laws that actually require landowners to control prairie dogs on their property.

Scientists estimate that 98 percent of all prairie dogs that existed during the 1800s have been exterminated. The Mexican prairie dog is now an endangered species, the Utah prairie dog is almost endangered, and many believe that the widespread black-tailed prairie dog will soon be endangered, too.

The little Utah prairie dog is now very rare due to hunting, poisoning, and the destruction of its wild prairie habitat.

CUT OFF

Most of the surviving prairie dog towns are quite small, and cut off from other prairie dog towns by farmland, roads, and other buildings. This means that they cannot mate with members of other colonies, which can lead to health problems from **inbreeding.** Smaller towns can also be destroyed very quickly by outbreaks of disease like **sylvatic plague,** or catastrophes such as flash floods. When this happens, it is not just the prairie dogs that suffer. All the animals that rely on them for food suffer, too. The hawks, eagles, foxes, badgers,

Like many prairie hunters, the kit fox has become scarce now that prey animals like prairie dogs are much less common. Predators always disappear earlier than their prey.

black-footed ferrets, and other **predators** that **prey** on prairie dogs have to find something else to eat. And as the prairie dog **lawns** become overgrown and the brush takes over, the animals that live on them have to move out. According to scientists, the life cycles of close to 150 different **species** are connected in some way to the prairie dog.

VANISHING WILDLIFE
Many animals that have always lived alongside prairie dogs are in deep trouble. The burrowing owl is

Over thousands of years the mountain plover has come to rely on prairie dogs because the lawns of their towns make good nesting sites.

becoming rare, and both the swift fox and the black-footed ferret are likely to be listed as endangered species. The mountain plover, which nearly always nests on prairie dog lawns, is disappearing from the plains. Some scientists consider the loss of the prairie dogs close to a natural disaster because the effects on other wildlife are so severe.

HELPING HANDS

Luckily, some people are trying to help prairie dogs. Volunteers rescue them from land where they are not wanted, and release them in wild areas where they can live in peace. In Colorado, the cities of Boulder and Fort Collins have set aside large areas of grassland as prairie dog reserves. A city park in Santa Fe, New Mexico, has its own **colony** of Gunnison's prairie dogs. Wildlife reserves throughout the Midwest have healthy, growing prairie dog towns.

Many people think that ranchers should welcome prairie dogs on their land, too. In the past, wild buffalo made a point of **grazing**

Huge herds of cattle have replaced buffalo on many prairies. Many people believe that cattle should live alongside prairie dogs, just as buffalo did in the past.

around prairie dog towns because the grass was shorter and sweeter. Cattle might benefit from grazing around prairie dog towns in the same way.

Like the buffalo, the prairie dog is a native American and a part of the continent's history. The buffalo has been making a comeback in recent years, and hopefully the prairie dog will do the same.

HOPEFUL FUTURE

Today there is very little wild prairie left, so prairie dogs are never going to be as common as they used to be. There is just not enough room for them. But after over 100 years of habitat destruction, shooting, and poisoning, it seems that many people are changing their minds about these **burrowing** squirrels. Instead of being treated as pests, they are being seen as part of America's wildlife heritage—like the buffalo and the bald eagle, two other species that were threatened with extinction not long ago.

Grassland Allies

Scientists who study prairie dogs and their effects on the landscape believe that they actually improve the food value of grassland. As they dig through the soil they mix air into it. This helps **microbes** in the soil break down dead plants, returning their nutrients to the soil. The prairie dogs' droppings decay in the same way and work like **fertilizer.** A wide variety of grasses and **forbs** can grow in this rich soil, many of which contain vitamins that are important to the health of grazing animals. The constant nibbling stops the growth of long grasses and big, coarse plants. It also encourages the small plants to sprout new, tender leaves. So despite what the ranchers think, prairie dogs could be their best friends.

I DIDN'T KNOW THAT

Glossary

burrow to dig a hole or tunnel in the ground. A hole or tunnel used as an animal's home is called a burrow.

colonize to travel to a place where no one else lives and start a home there

colony group of animals living together

coterie smallest family unit within a prairie dog town or city, made up of parents and several generations of offspring

diastema gap between the front teeth and chewing teeth in rodents and many other plant-eating animals

ectothermic having a body temperature that stays about the same as the animal's surroundings

enamel hard covering on teeth

endothermic having a body that is able to regulate its own temperature using energy from food

extinct not alive anywhere

fertilizer substance that helps plants grow by providing them with important nutrients

forb broad-leaved plant; an important food source for prairie dogs

grazing moving from place to place to find and eat grass or other plants

hibernation to spend the winter in a special kind of deep sleep

horizontal in a direction that goes from side to side

inbreeding breeding between animals that are too closely related, which may lead to health problems

lawn area of chewed-down grass and plants around a prairie dog town; also any grassy area

mammal type of animal that is endothermic (warm blooded), has hair or fur, and nourishes its young on mother's milk

mature developed enough to breed; adult

microbe tiny living thing too small to see without a microscope

native belonging to a particular place

pioneer person that is the first to explore or live in an area

predator animal that hunts another animal for food

pregnant carrying a baby inside the body

prey animal that is hunted by other animals for food

rodent type of mammal that has long front teeth for gnawing, such as rats, mice, and squirrels. A prairie dog is a kind of rodent.

silica hard, glasslike substance. Blades of grass contain very small pieces of silica

socializing spending time with others

species group of organisms that share certain features and can breed together to produce offspring that can also breed

sylvatic plague disease carried by fleas that kills prairie dogs

territory area where an animal lives

trespass to enter another person's property (or animal's territory) without permission

ward part of a prairie dog town, made up of coteries, that keeps in loose contact with other wards

Further Reading

Baldwin, Carol. *Living in a Prairie*. Chicago: Heinemann, 2003.

Butterfield, Maria. *Animals on Plains and Prairies*. Chicago: Raintree, 2000.

Cole, Melissa S. *Prairie*. Farmington Hills, Mich.: Gale Group, 2003.

Craats, Rennay. *Black-Footed Ferret*. Minneapolis: Lake Street, 2003.

Crewe, Sabrina. *Life Cycles: The Prairie Dog*. Chicago: Raintree, 1997.

Patent, Dorothy Hinshaw. *Prairie Dogs*. Boston: Houghton Mifflin, 1999.

Staub, Frank. *Prairie Dogs*. Minneapolis: Lerner, 1998.

Index

Numbers in *italic* indicate pictures